Golden Strands
of
Bright Sunsets
with
Blue Echoes
of
Heart and Soul

Golden Strands

of
Bright Sunsets
with
Blue Echoes
of
Heart and Soul

<insert cover image>

William E. Dickinson

A painter of words

To order additional copies of this book, contact:
Xlibris Corporation
1-888-795-4274
www.Xlibris.com
Orders@Xlibris.com
70574

Table Of Contents

Peace, Faith, and Eternity

Venues Of Time

Dedication

To put beauty in heart
And love in soul
Seek God up above
And, make one whole

To those in harms way
In the cauldron of war
With conflict in the heart
For the freedom they adore

To the lonely in life's streets
With hunger in the soul
Feed with all our love
With this word or two my goal

William E. Dickinson, Author
And, painter of words

Golden Strands

They stream in all their vesture
These golden strands I see.
Flowing like pure sunlight
Down inspiration's path to me.

Through the pangs of darkness
They pierce that dark gray mass,
Encouraged by new mornings

They come to forever last
They dance on golden sunbeams
And play with tunes this day
Enveloping in quiet grandeur
Stretching minds with what they say

Enlightening and uplifting
With cogent terms and phrase
To brighten and enthrall,
Poetic sunbeams to brighten someone's day

Face Of Sorrow

You could see it in their eyes all that day
And hear it in their breath torn away
A sad and consummate hope and a prayer
Amidst their sorrow and ever-present care

Just beneath the surface
Flicking eyelids held it in
Those soft wet tears of compassion
My hand could hardly hold my pen

Their searing need for action
To search the many lists for a name
With golden pictures serenaded in a palm
Or a candle to light the flame

I only hope that those feet keep moving
To a place where someone knows
That the face of sorrow before them
Looks exactly like the last one showed

Faces Of Youth

The faces of youth flow on the tube
With duty and honor for families 'Viewed
Spectrums of hope and a future strong
Heroic results of a future now gone

Epic tales of commitment and trust
Gone in a flash-in a dusty crush
Overgrown the reasons why we are there
Suffice to say the results are unfair

For the portions dealt out in a no draft time
Where the poor and committed join the line
To a military machine second to none
It's hard to see their faces for some

Who wield the power and life's luxury
From safe homes and capitals without the need
For commitment, duty, and little pay
As the honor of serving is the heroes way

So I watch the names and the patriots in stripes
Shown on the tube, night after night
And, think of the wars where many have served
With sadness and thanks to the youth so deserved

Gift Of Friendship

The day in wisp of smoke
Is taken back in time
For days of sunlight can darken
In the ballad of life's decline

As the leaves of fall descend
Onto our homes, and the earth receives
Then the body's message trips
The descent of mortals to bleed

The oncoming of sad occasion
However natural its coming finds
The friends of the dear departed
Unto them our tears do bind

When memory mingles with smoke and sun
In darkness and pure light
And, friends no longer cross our path
In the beauty of friendship bright

Painter Of Words

My easel is a word, a phrase
My pen is color blue
The brush applies a tinge, or
Accents
A pointer, a clue

A palette wide ere consummate
It strangles time, nor space
Wide as imagination 'vast
To compliment line with grace

Idea, a drop of color
It splashes where it may
Widening as it spreads
From instant to a day

And, the canvass in 'Varied
Likeness
To a person, scene, or space
Inanimate of the painters
Slash
Imagination in a race

Love In Flight

The great kaleidoscope that is America
So well represented on Flight 93
Those willing, able, and so sadly bourn
On a flight of heroism and tragedy

A "melting pot" spanning life's spectrum of people
There unexpected passage lifted to a greater good
On a destination's unchartered journey
Beyond what life's evil realm ever could

So many stories of so many lives
Called upon lifting love to the skies
Knowing this love in so many ways
Lifted higher on that fateful heart stopping day

Their families with their actions on safer ground
Left alone, but left so proud
And, our country indebted to all of them
Flight 93 onto rainbows end

Honor no more can be
Than love for all given in sacrifice for we
Who live below their flight path strewn?
On the hearts of all Americans unknown

Banality

The wisdom of the ages lost
On temperate shores of languid thought
Where aspiration bound on righter mean
This noun proclaims its ultimate seam

When end so rightly adjust a mean
Where acid tossed cleans and reams
Away the slag of other world
Where 'Visions above you swirl

As plough runs through and newer seed
Its shell so old on rock it's cast
And, planning deep in wound to draw
So straight its blinders away-not saw

Good that's known and hears
Thrown on heap with tattered shears
Excalibur sword did not find
Banality, as heaven sought error thine

Arrow straight and true you have
To shatter all with diverse adds
Dimension mired in muddy sand
Quickly tossed into hells hand

Soft Rain

Falling soft as a feather
Light as the dew in spring
Caress the skin of heart
The lightness of a soul to sing

Intonation glides on a breeze
Comes from soul's inn to please
Our consciences depth that pines
Where the strings of hearts are entwined

Hear the light of fawn in wood
Beauty's grasp of all that is good
Agile shadow in perfect peace
Extol the 'Virtue of soul's release

Free the insight of grace instilled
From great and 'vast unknown hill
Which stores the light of sun beneath
Fortune of right near bequeaths

So, feather, breeze, and fawn of wood
As delicate as a lovers look
To place the soft summer rain
Into one's heart, again, again.

Canvass

I am but a canvas
On which to paint the world
In haughty multi-colored
Deft strokes, bold, yet . . .
Demure in corners unfurled

A stroke dashed in solid oils
Or a watercolor's flowing seas
With gentle caress of pen with ink
Catch blush of girl for me

Now! Darker hue for red line
Drawn, the heart does bleed
From love, or hate, or anger
In the eye, or soft. hearts need

This finger touches the pen, or knife
Consoling digits exclusive right
Which brush-stroke flung, or slide
Canvass of life expose or hide

Now, see the name on bottom right
In splash of colors diminished light
Beyond a heart, or soul
Is a characters one true White Night to hold.

The Quiet Times

The quiet times envelop in a sweet nostalgic fog
The dampness being friendly and the noiselessness a rod

Running through my consciousness with a gait
strong and true
Carrying through it all until tumults are disarrayed
in my quiet rule

Of thought which conception carries on a tide
and a wave to shore
Where the immigrant of my mind can find
the haven it adores

Away from my days involvement, or the riptide of dissent
Where the orderly become unruly even though
love is always sent

Not to take away that one of conception, which comes
in the quiet of the night
Where concentration is most easy
where the quiet times are my light

Memorials Absorbed

The Jaws of Life grasped my soul
Amalgamated my thoughts
Sadness found it's home
While the minds conscience rolls

The feelings of the many dead combine
From an Agent Orange or mushroom haze
Exhausted in imagery, flung
In its metric yet cubic lines
Look again into the depth
Of its flat dark face
Can conscience be defined?

The foot, one after one
Follows; stone away from stone
I stoop and lay my imagery
On the combined sadness
Of thousands, and I am not alone

That epic struggle with death
Through muddy streets,
Hills and the skies of freedoms hope
Continues its fanciful, trendy, haunting ways
In a constant tide of emotions
Cast on a beach of quicksand
To retreat and ebb away

You say I cannot even know
The wider, older entity
That is the composite
A requisite of times emissions
That clearing of the shackles
Of recent dead immunes
The contrite conscience

The inhibitions of youthful zeal
That is intellects reflection
Enlarging inquisitions in the fourth dimension
They solidify, and that;
"Long sad marble stone"** overcomes!

Is the job done in this
Erection to sacrifice?
Away, home, now and then
So the sadness may have
Meaning and allay the fears
Of a living demise
With a trembling hand
They scratch a name

** From: The poem, A Place To Rest

Unobtainable Reach

It had all started with a broken back.
The bare spot to high for my stretching paintbrush.
Now, a fall and recuperation at home.
A blank pad of white paper, open, intimidating, then the idea!
With the idea imbedded-the title was easy!
Are not we all seeking it? Wisdom in our own way?
The Title: "The Wisdom Seeker" Three years and many
revisions later.
Critiqued by a friend, it was finished.
That was the easy part. The selling was a bit harder!
Everyone seemed to like it, even a famous Martial Artist!
His company had a big backlog of material
Two Subsidy Publishes liked it for very nice fees.
I let it sit, stored in a place in my heart.
Pushed the poetry again, and Nominated Poet Of The Year.
Didn't get it three times, another publisher contacted me
for a story
The process took three years, then nothing, nothing!
All checks in mail, then nothing. Unobtainable reaches
all of them.
This hopeless writer wrote novel two, a sequel.
In the two years waiting for novel #1 to get published
Was my third fall, a fall from life's ladder.

Henchmen Of Time

I, a bitter man lost and so forlorn
Yet, the time to tell erst while
Is not on my agenda else to form

The bowels of earth opened up
And, lost my heart deep inside
This cavernous sanctity of loss
Swallowed time and elicits soul to bide

These eons preying on mortality
Slogging over nearest hill
To grasp my conscience, numbing
I need a wayward still

And gargle contents incessant proof
Yet gracefully to age
Then drink the cup of ageless time
Whose potency portends the sage
A master not of mine

So, now the henchman gathers up
All accumulations of binding lost
And, I the arbiter not the priest
Yet, still I pay times cost

White Steel

It's hoary white grasp
Clutch at eyes, and nose, and mouth
The tentacles of cold
Crept, even as an icy sting
From face to hands
To the body's cold storage

With allusive beauty,
And deadly gate
It rambled, shook, and tore
At the human, and his remnants
Of sanctity that was futile to the core

As its grip of white steel
Encircled, covered, and froze
The powerful and vain were humbled
For, natures white mace
Had stifled, cajoled, and beaten man's inner abode

This blizzard of 98 once again
Instilled the smallness that is man
Into a rigid arrogance that he
Is merely another animal in nature's solid realm
to withstand . . .

Diana's Heart Of Love

Not only the sadness of the dying
Nor the pain of the living hurt
In that emulsifier of cruelty
Contained in the world she tried to skirt

Could transform this lovely lady
From her heart to wondrous love
Into the demons who pursued her
In their churlish riveting shoves

Her beauty of the facial
Belied her depth and space
For the humbled and downtrodden
Which she lifted with her grace

Now, with knowing loss this beauty .
Will skirt the world in space
As an angel for the poor and hungry
Whom she sponsored face to face

So, good-bye to this lovely lady
In her reign, which only now is free
With loving memories your beauty shines on
Over a world now left at sea

Face

I saw the face of God one day
Depicted on the dead who lay
With smile, contentment on journeys run
This other life in heavens noon days sun
Amid hope and lesser things which be
Our mortal fallacies flowing free
Encompass traditions of heritage long
As Chinese cups exquisite form

In culture through warring tribes did flow
Dynasty perfected our thoughts in throws
Where upheaval followed by harmony's theme
Progressed through age to age-archives keen

To learn this culture new world amazed
In fabled heritage throughout its days
Of toil and torment in 'vast land some flew
On wings of liberty from homeland drew

A face of change as dynasty's frame
A picture book of love and shame
As epoch tale through time and 'verse
Shadows cling to face, as sun is a light burst

Symposium

They gather and are heralded
In the hope and space of time
With the quick step of the ode
These poets from many lands so fine

With the courage of their convictions
Espoused from so deep within
The essence of a life's dream
That constant conviction; a hymn

With pens so sharp in morning
Evening or deep in the night
No day to pass without a thought
I will surely get it right

So, on the plug the 'Verses
Shakespeare had his day
Perhaps my next line will finish
This poem in which my heart will stay

Embedded so 'Very deep within
The spirit, heart and soul of me
Flushed in mindset cast in gold
If only the lines are eternity

Rivers Of Steel

I wander in lack-luster
The deaden stools of night
As I sit among the layers lost
In infinities endless might

The progression of inequities banner
Flown above the crowd
In the deadening quiet of justice-left
Lost among ones crowd

I see the tender waters harden into steel
Flowing down the alleyways
Of ambitions dangerous zeal

And, then the constant hammering
Of prejudice playing cards
Thrown against the table-betting
Can't allay that hardening heart

Now, all the rivers strands once bright
Piercing heart, hope, and soul
This red rusts corrosive change
Into rivers of human steel
A mindset so very, very cold

Thought Path

I am but a traveler
No time in warp abide
Here on mother earth, confined
Myself, no other rely

No other, but creation
Emission of mind's intent
A vast world of inner soul
Eclectic, maroon, not spent

Rainbow in its ocular taste
With many hews, some gold
A mixing of the basic ones
Some solid mixtures, bold

Languid mind, interrupted,
Engulfed
Flood down path conception
Dictates, controls
Follow the fever rush, rush of red
Rich blood, the thought
Unfolds

Dance On Tomb

The clean white sun as laughter danced
On the pillage of a mind encamped
Upon the soft red velvet of a bloodless war zone
That which the warriors are self with sufferance revamped

"Unto the children of God came the anointed"
With the art of Sun Tzu's war unknown repulsed
So inertia inscribed the warrior screaming

And the lamb lay down with the tiger
With the quiet of an interminable spirit
Two in one beyond the cataclysmic horizon
As the yellow ball of acceptance rose

With the legions muffled charge
Alone the spirits of quelled giants on the winds
Distant seeds as washed dreams blowing in dew
Iridescent in diffused dancing light

Onto the tomb of the giant warriors last breath
Self rises to dance in special light
His hollow breath in pain subsides in pensive harmony
As the tomb of defeat swirls

Through the mist of dawn and evening
With the sword of Michelangelo as harbinger
Riding "The Four Horses Of The Apocalypse"—crying
Who is this "Painter of Words?" Only silence!

Veins Of Grace

A feather in the wind
Stilled by lack of breeze
Retains its lightness, beauty
Allowing eye to see

Its delicate veins of grace
The sunlight through to view
Allowing wind to pick up again
Into constant movement, new

Now, into air aloft
Framed by the big blue sky
Movement untamed
Light projectile
From ground it now tries . . .

And, gathers its momentum
Blowing as a gale
Movement as a friend I know
Although she's just
A little pale

Beauty Of The Moment

Beauty sweet, intrinsic, or beauty sweet of sight
The great value of heart with soul so meek, so right
Nature flows before us, this almighty gift to all
And beauty from the heart, perhaps by God installed

As soul unknown, yet far it's reach
With heart defines the friend
Unceasing in all its love
From above, and deep from within

Accept with all its fractions often mired in doubt
Dig below confusions reign, and pull away that doubt
And believe in all humanity, where Christ has gone before
Certainty of nature's beauty brings God closer to our core

Believe in all humanity, although often sad and frayed
With love and soul in all of us, let this beauty be displayed
This beauty of the moment and beauty from the sky
Let it always come forth, and see ones soul arise

Antiquities Nest

Low the bat eared archives roam
The lonely hill of wants bad ills
Intellectual library and facts demise
Lonely epochs of man and natures disguise

Man s rise and fall in saddened tears of the lost
Where wars, strife, solutions, and errors lurk
These plaintiffs eye shelved stories unattended
Left for time and man to read and dread

Fallout and fortitude rest on lower shelves
Where dust and knowledge rest
Unchecked, unwanted value lost
On those who have no check

Ambition within fiery page now dead
Solutions lay in slack solitude
Only shadowed leaders give them bed
New tears wash new lies into old catacombs of servitude

In death, old and new heroes are paged to antiquity
The wisdom of ages past, lost anew
Where the bank of knowledge waits in muted deliverance
And, where the bank of epochs awaits the insightful few

March 11, 2007

Mixed Virtues

Sense and scene of triumph found
Accolades and errors doom
Patriotism, faith, and honor bound
Where do sensibilities have room?

Without support save innate self
The poor and hungry amidst the war and chaos
Forgotten in the midst of strife
Abused by governments, allegiances, man, and nature

Targets as instruments of change
As mere numbers on the lists of hate
Maligned as inconsequential backwaters
Surviving on their own basic native intelligence

The stench of poverty, hunger, and anonymity
Amidst power hungry survivalists
Controlling factors in many other hands
The good as well as the extremely bad

Darfur, Iraq, Afghanistan, Palestine, a few
Others controlling destinies as they die
As the world looks on in sadness
Unable or unwilling to help these "depleted masses"

Beauty

Beauty, is it in the "eye of the beholder"
A lovely affliction of the eye
Such a true sense of ones being
For: It is the best a heart buys

What pleases the sense of what we are?
Defining the unknown pleasure which satisfies
High on the impact of one's senses
That which nothing can take away

A lovely face, demeanor, or action
A gesture, which embodies help
A lonely pursuit of truth or justice
A known or unknown penchant for loving all things-felt

The smile of beauty as conscience
Natural act without effort or malice
Beholden only to feelings displayed
Or, held within the hearts warmth as chalice

On the sunlit morning of a perfect day
When all is right with God and man
Employing some goodness within
Enrapturing the eye, mind, or heart to warm

March 10, 2006

Natures Quieter

Fall down; fall down yea soft, soft mode
Beyond my ken and mood
Light and fluffy so, so smooth
Eclipse man's soul and sooth

Lassitude and languish gone to bed
Soft blown beyond my alien stoops
Shovel handy but not in grasp
Fallacies of power suddenly droop

Epitome of latent songfest mutes
Into softness all is gone
Into great white quiet
Softened node alights on home and lawn

Man's great power now muted
Soft friend has come in night
From 'Valleys of sky's immeasurable depth
Allay our sins in white

Pure wet fingers from the north
Have settled far and wide
A poster of a hand above
Wet nurture for us to abide

March 13, 2007

Community

The flowing hand of time and space
Inequitable in its diverse ways
Allows an infinite range of emotion
In a cascade of tears
And hope sometimes defrayed

Where a community of good people
Can come together along God's way
Unknown all paths and tributaries
The gracious hand of community
In his hands to shepherd us on these days

Down, Down, Down

Down, down, down
It came
The water and the mud
Drown, drown, drown
Sad times
The sadness, agony, blood
From inside the crater
Flowed
Mud, mud, mud
The houses, people, animals
On smallest patch
They stood, stood, stood
On the roofs of houses
They waited in despair
Until the helicopters came
And, plucked them
Into the air
Now, the world can help
With care, care, care

So Much To Love

The depth of human kindness
Beyond the grasp of most
The "wholly owned subsidiary" of heart
To warm a soul as host

We see it in the small things
The large ones follow through
With some it is ingrained so deep
Close to the Holy Ghost to 'View

Effortless these deep, dear instincts
The few it finds to grind
A drive, acumen long imbedded
This "fallacy" of kind

Fallacy only in those outcomes lost
A litany of sadness—he bears the cost
Yet, a better man few have met
When kindest man pays all life's debts

Perhaps tight balance be one of these
When good the all consuming leaves
His burdened task far up above
Where he did get so much to love

Cross Of Ages

Cross of ages cleave to me
As terror lays brutal ash on we
Who on this new world of sin
With the exasibated face of agony not so thin

Appears on face of traveler bourn
On new age of terrors horn
Whose trumpet of death with suspicion lay?
Across the tracks of feet in clay

Absorb this time with terrors plight
Nations history destroyed that might
Of fascists fest on night of fear
Dispelled by gritty Brit so dear

Nine, eleven, seven is it to combine our worth
To bring terror to its knees
Bye virtue, honor, bound in all
In this entire world this terror falls and flees

From vigilant strengths of good in world
Whose affection and love must hold?
All groups, creeds, and ethnic needs
To bosom of honest truth must feed not fold

Two Shorelines

Epoch reminders of nature's realm
True measures of winters grasp
White caked ice along miles of shore
Along white beaches as
Lonely reminder of summers past

Deep blue cold of changing sea
Beyond this frozen helm
Promise of new "arctic fleece"
Toward the shores untold sum

The eyes of untold access
Beyond the sheen of now
Present the fathomless depths
Of winters strutting prow

Angelic voice in wind not heard
Whistle down the winter's pike
How long the smothered sea to last
Beyond two shorelines bay tonight?

February 12, 2007

Feather Light Life

When the demons of antiquity
Evolve to the present time
Then sad, dark fears of evil
Come down the road to thine

Though the spirit of humanity
Checkmates the spreading vein of dark
With the wonderment of giving
Of love from those sweet folk with sparks

With the core of humane feelings
Where all deep down abide
With the basic decent bonding
When tragic circumstances come neigh

Our "feather light lives" each morning
Such a precious commodity
The loving one to the other
Circumstance brings us closer
To our own humanity

April 17, 2007

Wider Pathways

The world of wider pathways
From our own internal strife
Quiescent in perceived quiet moorings
Alone they give no life

Flow greater this unction foreword
And gird our powers to land
Beyond the ken of self and country
Into the good of Promised Land

Low the great full promised dome
The lucky and the vetted
Of privileged promised house
Where vision is never met

On this fabled road and pathway
Where the Lord's tiles of roof are made
With the heavenly houses awakening
And our shallowness is put in shade

Purple veins of latent events
Constrict our most valiant thoughts
Where the blood of Christ inhabits
So true intent won't be for naught

March 6, 2007

For Same

I look upon the urban mass
Of mistakes and faults in life
My own little compilation bound
Into its own little maze of strife

And that chancey lady called, The Lucy One
Which most times has ignored
Yet, her sister, Pure Physicality
Is the one that really adored

The lonely aspects of one's life
Those ones pure chance does 'Vet
On that street called mortality
It's lonely-yet not met

So, find a great ambition
Always waning in the wind
Is it really so important
When grim reaper doesn't enter in

Thanking the almighty one
From which all of this came
Wondering what great purpose
We all must do for same

Winters Return

The sleeping hand of God
Awakens ones soul to peace
In a fabulous white dimension
Enabling all to see

The beauty of the ages
Enveloping all in white
Soft reflection brings to term
The foolishness of God to fight

Nature in all its vastness
In showers overshadowing all
Mans ego and puny attributes
He gave them all to fall

Into his own reflection
In a Trinity of power and might
With a softness in resplendent flakes
To make over mind in purer light

Soft, soft descending moisture
To nourish mind, soul, and earth
In the wonders of creation
So human caretakers get a second birth

March 16, 2007

Foreign

What is the paragon of virtue?
That to which we all ascribe
That infinitesimal mirage of hope
That we all can reach for the sky

Is it to foreign to be ladled?
Out as from a font
As our pre-judgment of the unknown
A scary thought that haunts

Vision just a mind-set
To which the good and bad
Are comfortably chronicled, cancelled
To a vision we can grasp?

Nightmare always ready
When the subject is unknown
To fill the empty spaces
When ignorance is full blown

Difference is an enemy
When unable the aspect sees
The other is the same
Unique, an individual as you and me

Dawn Of Ages

Cogent man imbued in thinking lay
Those scattered seeds to wisdoms day
Experience entrenched in genomes bay
As heralds banner amid apoplectic ways

Ensconced the fallowness of past
Spirits drifting forward with myths remembrance cast
Gifts of God's or devils rug underfoot
Lowly quagmire under these annals hood

As listless sloth progress foot by foot
Animal instincts survival slowly could
The affirmation of heralds, sorcerers, and mystic beasts
Underfoot of presents slowly creep

Eons come and blue green jades
A spectrum all and not have made
Beyond, behind, dwelt in 'Vine
Of progress, dispassionate juries out, finds

Dark black jet of transients' multicolored rays
Which art that imbued in holy or pedantic ways
Alluvial soil on sands of time
Who art thou, or not to find

From The Heart

I write of tepid, limpid things
And then, there are great events
Human emotion strung on high
To float through ethos vent

Imagination as real true friend
It comes when blank the page
Extolling virtues in mass beyond this elf
In quirky, allusive, beautiful ways

When all around sad human events
Play on mind and say . . .
This story must be told in verse
Beginning or ending life's play

Hopefully absent though sorrow found
In hearts, and souls, and eyes
From age to age emotion takes
Great leaps though, with hope one relies

Through life's dripping pen in blood and tears
Sometimes blot page, soul, conscience, and heart
Just a painter of words pen in hand
For a Poet it's just his part

Heroic Warriors

The firestorms of all battles gone
Sadness left with taste of fire
Eloquent symbols and courage strewn
Will the hope of freedom still inspire?

Nation of peace in war-torn times
Gathering storms be yours or mine?
Allocations responsibility unable to portend
The olive branch as enemy or friend!

Conflicted options in these irrational times
Soldiers and governments on the line
Men and women of action always serve
Hoping judgments are a sweet dissert

Giving all to the end
Lasting friendships always send
Comradeship often the only way
Lasting through wars tumult each day

Country, family, enemy, friend
Why do wars never end?
Consequence, consideration, depth in thought
Hoping leaders consider the "knots"

Infrastructure, fracture, societies of old
Beyond the presents immediate goals
Training, basic, cultures, institutions unknown
Perhaps better intelligences will bring heroic warriors home

May 28, 2007 (Memorial Day)

I Believe

I believe in the infinite
And, in God to trust
How else this vast dominion
Beyond life's grain and rust

The scientist and noble scholar
In depth beyond their sums
Invincible image in lofty vogue
Awaits beyond them comes

Emotion a forgotten equation
Assumption, myth, and sight
Beyond life's great allusions
Or, a destiny is our fright

Explain the wandering canorous
Delve into the night of sums
Collegial balance lost in rhyme
Unknown life's values run

Into the unexpected
Or, thrown the way of fate
That arbiter of coincidence
When thrown on many plates

Extol the virtuous ambience
Thrown on "Saint El'mo's fire"
That breather of abundance
Not caustic but inspired

Inevitable Overlapping

The infinity of coincidence
In life's layers of understanding
In infinite manifestations of culture
Within perceptions irony of flame

Time honored customs of unknown 'Visage
Placated into unions of misunderstanding
Total fabric layered on creased intelligence
Wire worn these creases on velvet assumptions

Credence like fore thought not Priest or official
The individual a planner in open plains
Wind of change beholden to none
Apolitical empathy a soulless grace

Amalgamation of pathos the order of day
Nights the antithipass of wrath
Virgin soil not in this realm
These merging shadows of the spook

Where fore are these bizarre dimensions
The eye to spy on nurtured nest
Overwhelming ambiguities in guise of one
Washington Father of country or nemesis as city?

Kiss And A Tear

In an explosion of deadly malice
A kiss of life with a tear
Enabling a long arduous journey
Back to family, friends, a renewed career

Vignettes of lifelong loveliness
With hope, and wife Lee as a loving friend
A wile with hope and presence
His voice from the past alive again

Lady luck a friend in need
With kids a teacher taught
The best of medicines practitioners
And a zest to beat the odds

Long those odds of recovery
For soldiers, marines, and all
These heroes who like Bob
Hope to recover for service given for us all

February 27, 2007

Land Of Freedom

A gracious land of freedom
Seems to settle in the mire
When her accolades are stilted
By events when fallible men inspire

Masses of men and institutions
Corporations and governments into
Hysteria of acquisitions
The power of large being the only new

Where the end justifies any mean
In the guise of heavenly glow
And the future with the past
Is a concentric circle in the brightness of their glow?

In the trading of their vision
Short sighted and power bent
Collateral damage not considered
And, the truth is really bent

Behind all facades and pretensions
The hardest core of right intent
Diminishing hard fought rights and sacrifice
Over all the years our freedom sent

The sweaty brow of true communion
In the God fearing upward climb
Where truth, honesty, and hard work
With the tenets of the loving and the kind

Life's Maze

I see not the white cloud coming
Only the fallacy of our days
In muted sounds of redemption
Playing on the harp of broken ways

Beguiling anthems of tribute
Allay our faulted maze
Entwined within our physiology
In plodding steps to see more grace

Absolute in all outpouring
Is certain numbness toward the end?
Where frequent stops and hesitations
Leave a mark toward what we portend

Invigorating the world so sinful
Are captured moments set ablaze?
When humanity, God, and nature
Become the journey through life's maze

Extol those wondering, alabaster times
When our insight and God collide
Into that wonderment of true believing
If that white cloud clearing the fog in our way decides

March 4, 2007

Light Encounter

New sight is a light encounter
When sight so far can see
The 'Vision 'Vast that satisfies
My occult of satisfaction please

That great journey long fashioned
By our maker of the Gods
Who mankind the instinct satisfies
Accept, not really rob

Yet, when that gift faulters
Vision not really wide
Slowly, away it goes
We see the darker side

Beyond the "Ancient Mariner"
Over scope of sea did roam
Floating overseas so 'Vast
He always was at home

If locked away on island
Constriction would endure
And, slowly sight is focused
No 'Vision beyond one shore

Metamorphic Dreams

They come as dreary messengers
In the nights of ambience lost
Within the swagger of unknown heights
Ablaze with the hear-after unknown costs

Dancing and dazing realities memories
Until the augment of daylights recovering lesions
Not brutal the impact, but a shearing blow
Even as the nights battle is mist not to know

Where in the drudge of another day
It's onset preprogrammed in its usual ways
Not dazzling with magnanimous authority
But, the friendly sameness all preconceived

The delights of dawning differences
Not, the alabaster rays of the present's realm
Prescribed with times allotted hands
Not foe, but holding all the known

More friendly as the cup hits the lip
Of resurgent realizations awakening
To the beams of intent and purpose
Arising, letting the metamorphic dreams disappear

BLUE ECHOES

Silent Echoes

The flags of love have flown away
Life's lonely hole remains
Manifesting hours in wondering
Why legions of naught gain

Spirit, look, and instant
All pass to big, blue sky
Where the hollow sound of nothing
Like fall leaves leave heart so dry

Silent echoes rebound in heart
As look of starry eye
A vaunted chasm much to wide
When cold anonymity does now arise

No friendly little gestures
Or, look to say, "hello"!
Is depth so shallow of feeling
What is it I don't know?

I close the box on issues
When a tear is strained to fall
Emotion in a whirlwind
Now I walk down empty halls

All life's dreams are scattered
Into the realm of outer space
Now the cooling wind of winter
Leaves splendor disheartening fall in place

William E. Dickinson
A painter of words
(To the winds cast.)

Emotions Turn

What is the essence of a life
When tides of emotion loom?
Like fragile feathers flown before
To land or be flown under loves new moon

When emotions apex comes in tides of love
Or crashes in powerful waves recall
Is sparkle in eye renewed
Or, dulled—all light to fall?

Caustic embers in the eye
Covers looming fear
How can sparkle shine through this
When doubt is always near?

In cage of haunting loneliness
Lovely bird outside is seen
With beauty beyond redemption
Cages cruelty is a means

Within these bounds we function
Necessities first hour is grim
Truncated appetites immersed
As showers of tears fall in

William E. Dickinson
A painter of words
September 12, 2009

Lost Dreams

Entranced and intrigued
Beyond redemption
Standing alone
In the nether land

Entering the valley of denial
I am denied the hearts recognition
With possibilities infinity laid to rest
In the quicksand of illusion and mist

Florid happiness floating
Floating into the sea of despair
Dreams as illusion understood
As hope, love, affection, even friendship?
All in abeyance unrecognized

William E. Dickinson
A painter of words
September 3, 2009

Over The Lamplight

Over the lamplight
My stolen heart does wander
Between the beams
As a fallen star

Interest, awakening the heart
Responds as player
In a sea of allusion
The tempests and valleys to come

A beam of light from soul
Bounces out in hopes delight
An aging nemesis
Behind the bones of the past

The beam train taken
Unknown source or destination
Only, the marked entity
Of transition—who laughs aloud

Dour aspects alight the passenger car
Joined by comic release
Sitting at the lunch counter
Of delight are disparaging anecdotes

Disillusionment, disbelief, and despair
A little songbird held in their arms
Singing her release
And, capture from love

The songs not heard
By the souls beam
As the train of life
Seeks boundaries known

All beams fade into shadows
Warmth and light gone
The fading beams stilled
Paint a thousand words of dust

William E. Dickinson
A painter of words
July 7, 2009

Tranquil Union

I sit in tranquil union
As the day's beauty is to close
And, think of all the others
Who may not be exposed

To the wonders of nature
Where man has stepped aside
And allowed this flowing beauty
To in our hearts reside

As the wonders of creation
Maintained in God's estate
Where heart and soul in union
Are the best which we can make

And, those conflicts in our hearts
Dispel with soft cool breeze
The moment we understood
Not all these days will please

As tumults of man and nature
Are a part of life's track
Down our road in a journey
Which God alone has stacked

To be our trial and fortune
Of love, death, and strife
Beyond the middle road
Of love and death in night

On our journey of discovery
The mind and heart to fend
Off all lonely discourse
To love all as new friends

The warp in our foundation
Is different man and child
As we overcome
Many obstacles and smile

Perhaps, journey is the outcome
And life is the test
As we progress forward
To become our very best

In this tranquil union
Of trial and soul of man
With peace and love for all
And, journey in God's hands

William E. Dickinson
A painter of words
October 5, 2009

Wistful Wind

Life, as wistful as the wind
Time in observance
Given in God's faith
To hold and cherish

That emblem of each soul
Held within
God's hope and treasure
That in his hand we move

So that when life is done
As that wistful wind
Through the trees of life
The journey nourishes soul

Then agony as a fleeting moment
Is taken away and dispersed
Into heavenly white clouds
From heaven

And, the stilled heart
Regains life hear-after
With God and man
Unto eternity

William E. Dickinson
A painter of words

BRIGHT SUNSETS

A Light Ticking

This lovely morning of hope
Elastic with its promise for the day
Widening as the sun expands
Our hearts soft with the upcoming rays

The tick of a clock my only companion
Awaiting, even as I, the large hands of God moving
Excalibur, the slicing sword to come
Dividing digits of life into mine

With effortless accumulation its space graduates
It's sunny companion warming the hands
Gently grasping the light of the day to come
Unfolding together into my day

I, just a partner along for times ride
Observing with slow anticipation
The beating of spaces progression
Not the master of warmth or time

Slow inexhaustible time and light
My friends this early mourn
Progressing, warming, flowing into another day
As the mere "painter of words" scratches in unison

Eternal Warmth

True loves death
Never comes
Residing in tranquil memory
It caresses the soul
Forever holding fast
In times memory
All that was and is good
Keeping pleasant hostage forever
Loving times kept
In the hearts eternal warmth

William E. Dickinson
A painter of words

Feathered Lights

My sordid heart does ponder
The light now in my eyes
Banished to the night time
Where a sad and lonely tale arise

The decade of a lifetime
Gone as beauties rays
Sunk below the ocean
I thought had end my days

If a little song bird
Gentle as the dew
Flew into my life
Would beauty be renewed

Will the tears in life continue
As I know not of the fears
The mysteries of life continue
Perhaps a mastery without cheer

Yet, when a feather lights
No impression does it leave
In life we dance about
Beauties light is there—indeed
Maybe, our only need

William E. Dickinson
A painter of words
March 20, 2009—2:30 am

Glorious Reflections

What the heart does
Is nobody's world
That slip between the pages
Of time left in mist

That, all-bite, partially gone
Almost there, indefinite
Fragile, like lead stained glass
Ready to break, or to mold

Reflections scattered, some lost
Clouds outside with the cherubs and goblins
Inside the glorious anthems music
Of the souls presence and hearts longing

Angel dust collecting on prisms of colored panes
Yet, the sun in the frozen north
Not penetrating clouds of disillusionment
Yet, a single ray comes through

Striking the ancient glass of time itself
Back through the clouds of wonderment
Reflections clearing
With the morning sun

And, the stained glass
Alights inside and outside
As lovely voices are heard
Then, calligraphy's heart responds

To lighten a day,
Just Bill painting words

FACE OF WAR

Face Of War

+++++++++++++

The scarred face of war on page
With limpid protestations from power bade
Necessary there sacrifice for good
On war the mighty never understood

Clean the office, Oval or #10
Decisions made for heartier men
To fight the good fight proclaimed so true
Through histories archives on war is a dirty brew

This sordid mess of rights—more wrongs
For, once it starts no easy pills can qualm
The passion, outrage, heroism, or death
As plague of blood on all are spilled and rest

Beyond the present where bodies lay
Onto the page and minds for days
Weeks, months, and years to come
Petrifying everything, and always one

Person by person, and mind for mind
Tainting, turning, revolving all kinds
Scarring the face of all that are left
Remembering the quagmire—always wars dead

William E. Dickinson
A painter of words
April 03, 2003

Cambridgeshire Crew

On a field not vast but dedicated, serene
Lies a place of valour and honour supreme
A unique cross on friendly Britain's Isles
"The Cambridge Cemetery For American's" miles

The throes of war have left it cleaned
By duty, honour, and freedoms vision seen
When crewmembers flew over foreign shores
Testing waters of faith—washing fascists hate
Clean to the core

Across many miles they came
With American faces and American names
Marking a place for a cross on North Slope of a hill
And a vista over woodlands to Ely Cathedral

The Memorial Chapel of Portland stone like St. Paul's
Teakwood doors and "Air Assault" on the walls
With decorations for valour above the main door
Depicting great honour and memories much more

For the gallantry of names outside these doors
In Cambridgeshire England are in peace they adored
This legacy of service of American women and men
As the sun sets over Old Glory again
And, the silence of history remembers when

William E. Dickinson
A painter of words
May 9, 03

Cathedral Of Hope

+++++++++++++++++

I could feel the thunder coming
And hear the ramparts call
That cloud of doubt 9/11 thick
It choked the breath from my saviors call

A great transformation engulfed me
As the towers of idealism died
With the strength of ascending heroes
And the sadness of the lost souls cries

This edge of despair was softened
In the captivating search by rough hands
While the compassion in all the helping
Made the loss almost able to be manned

As relatives held candles in sweet communion
The flame of hope ever burned
In their hearts a cathedral over ashes
Praying for information at every turn

As we honor these fellow Americans
In transition through these tragic days
All those hands held in hope and healing union
Can guide us to love in so many, many ways

William E. Dickinson
A painter of words, September 6, 02

Cold Treasures

The infirmities of the soul at war
Enclose the mind and conscience in an iron web
Of caustic embrosia which settles
On the wind enveloping all in a deaths wish

The enibriazation of valour sustains immediacy
With the quick justification of rightful success
Until the blood of winning or losing dies
On the body bags of peace

The gallant fields of poppies and magpies
Surrender the dead in an apparition of winning
Though, cause and justice are tired words
When the cost is measured in lives

Who is bad when the bullet flies
And, who is good when it lands
"Evil is as evil does" is said by man
And, evil does have its word in death

So' what is the cry in the wilderness
When the gallant fight with valour for peace
In the name of war consequence remains
On honor, truth, justice, and always hope released.

William E. Dickinson
A painter of words
December 31, 2003

War As Saint

In the interim of a lifetime
With the accolades of a mass
The "home truths" of realities momentum
On the mighty finally crash

With the windstorm of self adoration
There is the glassy eye of fear
When successes prescriptions unfulfilled
Can no longer disappear

And, the fantasy of only two shades
On the white night of a crusade
Envelops the many worlds of a man
Idyllic optimism soon fades

And, the jury tainted maladies
With the sufferance of protected power
All the true worth of the masses
Is conscripted and devoured

Bye self righteous martial edicts
Knowing not the mettle of restraint
Or, the power of truth and right
Beholding only to the devils war as saint

William E. Dickinson
A painter of words

Flowering Moonbeam

I leach the field of emeralds
In my soulful heart
Beyond my ken to harvest
This foolish soul won't part

The antonym is playing soft
A theme I don't know
Beyond a Brahmin's wishes
My wandering does flow

Down the unknown highway
That one in the stars
This galaxy of mixed emotions
Mostly from the heart

The slipping of a moonbeam
Beyond the darkest cloud
As a familiar objects passing
Like a little bird in a crowd

Holding hands at midnight
With a fairy tale of naught
Slipping through the mind's filter
Into another vestige caught

A flowery grave awaits the dream
Which settles on light air
This floating not steadfast
It's calling is not heard

William E. Dickinson
A painter of words
June 01, 2009/Midnight

Love

The fodder of the ages
One we can't do without
A soft entitlement sought
Crashing loss if it's in doubt

Flaming eagles flown in wind
Softly enveloped into loves limb
Wrapped in to enfolding arms
So the tree of life may go on

Questions, answers, turn of mind
Stirring as that tree in wind
Answers sought where none may be
Wind has slowed, now, stilled the tree

Now the gloom of quiet rests
In the trees storied eagles nest
Where beak of power near heavens rake
Absent flight of love to take

Talons of inspirations grasp
To hold and feather loving to last
So shoe on ground to further make
The step from sky and ground to shake

That beady eye to laser beam
And focus, land, and love to stream
Upon that object still in wind
Where loves template of warmth flows from within

Heat now unifying devours
Moment of love without showers
Where earth and sky and tree in midst
Compliment the eagles tryst

Now sip of wine—not only one
A toast to heaven and the sun
Where warmth of union sees the day
When love has finally found its way

William E. Dickinson
A painter of words
March 2, 2009

Make A Heart Cry

I have no love to gather
Within my troubled breast
My heart is sore and tangled
Without a place to rest

This lonely heart does falter
When the tune of love comes by
As a woeful sound emerges
Which fills an open sky

A freehold house of wisdom
Thrown amongst no glee
For a parcel of arrows
Has found no place to be

As the warring of emotions
Flood the streets of fire
Heaven and death mingle
Into a forlorn pyre

The ashes of containment
Fill box on box
As the crux of love is crushed
And, my wandering love is lost

William E. Dickinson
A painter of words
(A termite of emotions)

Sinking Smile

A song bird nestles in my tree
Settling into a soft cover of moss
Branches reaching and extending
To hold this chico-dee in its embrace

Her amber waves of song
Echoing in beauties repose
With mature notes and new vibrations
In slight discordance of unknown magnitude

Does the quiet of the night sweetly greet?
Or, are several notes in abeyance?
Source as the ultimate quarry
Lassitude of one—poignancy the other

A wayfarer traveling in close vicinity
Her song a mellow caressing number
Enticing a smile from his rock like fascia
"Romancing the stone", and extracting a sword

Slicing the trees branches
The bird alights on the strangers arm
Notes bounce off the metal blade
Reverberations echoing into the darkest of night

William E. Dickinson
A painter of words
May 14, 2009

So Much To Love

The depth of human kindness
Beyond the grasp of most
The "wholly owned subsidiary" of heart
To warmth in soul as host

We see it in the small things
The large ones follow through
With some it is ingrained so deep
Close to the Holy Ghost to view

Effortless these deep, dear instincts
The few it finds to grind
A drive, acumen long imbedded
This "fallacy" of kind

Fallacy only in those outcomes lost
A litany of sadness—he bears the cost
Yet, a better man few have met
When kindest man pays all life's debts

Perhaps tight balance be one of these
When good the all consuming leaves
His burdened task far up above
Where he did get so much to love

William E. Dickinson
A painter of words

PEACE, FAITH, AND ETERNITY

Alights

It isn't much in the morning to see
A little bird that lands on a feeder for me
With the wave of a wing in majestic flight
Taking the wind and heart out of sight

Reappearing with the others of color
Plumage of feathers, bold and so stellar
Red, the Cardinals, a pair so bright
Proud and glorious they stand out in the night

Finches so gold, and purple for me
Yet, there's the little white Albino who doesn't flee
When the blue, or red, purple or green
Many the birds who enter the scene

But, the singular action transparent to see
The little white Albino is justification for me
The feeders are there for all to partake
Even the lonely Albino without a mate

A symbol of man, lonely out there
Where a complicated world doesn't seem to care
Christmas is different we all seem to go
Help our neighbors, so our Albino will grow

William E. Dickinson
A.P.O.W.

Americas Image

I see her shinning beauty
And, see her late mirage
Wonderful excitement brought
When her valued lineage is caught

When a hand held in splendor
Her accepting oath to command
On the footage of America
Our free and diverse land

We, who already have her
Must be, and always see
Her beauty refreshed with new bounty
For those, a citizen to be

So to join this great image
In these freedoms we all see
And, hold in all our hearts
The values made not free

With the blood and courage of the past uniting
The spirit of our land to be
A country for all the ages
This America, the land of the free

William E. Dickinson, Veteran
A painter of words
July 4, 2009

Caring

The essence of a moonbeam
Shines through the night
When the caring of God's love
Becomes our beam and sight

When our little bit of love
Expands and includes
The fractured, sad, and lonely
Who need God's food

As, our less than perfect
Lives themselves display
We all need some healing
So, together we must pray

That experiences and feelings
In many different lives
Put it all in context
Where all in God rely

On us all as soul-mates
With different talents of love
To help each other
Become more caring in God's love

William E. Dickinson
A painter of words
9/16/09

Dawn Breaks

The valleys heights are opened
Vision the pasts preserve
Or, the morning's delight
Unknown the days coming

Will clouds overshadow
The colorful grasses and heather?
Ground covered with natures abundance
Sunlight streaming down, as the anchor for life

The fields of flowers soft smells
Entice the lovely wind to blow
Heads of daffodils swaying in the breeze
In a cadence of God's making

Morning sounds overtaking silence
Is a conjunction to one's ears
Stealthy predators low in grass
There padded paws no mark on ear or ground

The urban jungle distraught in distance
Configuration and conflagration
Discordant yet reassuring
To human life a distant quality

William E. Dickinson
A painter of words
An early morning?

Door Of Eternity

Swinging wide before me
The abyss I don't know
All thumping, ringing accolades lost
With a vision I now must sow

The darkened ends of time ensue
With black bounds not hailed
A flirt of loneliness prevails
I see entities all full and so pale

A practiced sound of nothing
Wafts in from the deadened sky
Age-old reminiscences settling down
These pages now closed with a sigh

A fractured life now wants me
Without my love to guide the way
Her soft repose in heaven
Remains for eternity's stay

William E. Dickinson
A painter of words

Feathers Touch

The flowing art of beauty envelops
The souls transition
As the notes of lovely movement
A caress of the souls heart

Light touch this feathers flight
In the wind of time
Absorbent as cool, cool water
Pleasurable as a clouds passing

Never the caustic sanctions
Of the everyday
This flight away from
Incandescent as new day

Movement without action
In a dome of nothingness
A cord of notes infusing
The essence of relaxations rest

No drumbeats—no plodding
Just the light indefinable
It's own musical theme
Auditory pleasure supreme

Bill Dickinson
Just painting words

I Believe

I believe in the infinite
And, in God to trust
How else this vast dominium
Beyond life's grain and rust

The scientist and noble scholar
In depth beyond their sums
Invincible image in lofty vogue
Awaits beyond them comes

Emotion a forgotten equation
Assumption, myth, and sight
Beyond life's great allusions
Or, a destiny is our fright

Explain the wandering canorous
Delve into the night of sums
Collegial balance lost in rhyme
Unknown life's values run

Into the unexpected
Or, thrown the way of fate
That arbiter of coincidence
When thrown on many plates

Extol the virtuous ambulance
Thrown on "Saint El'mo's fire"
That breather of abundance
Not caustic but inspired

William E. Dickinson
A painter of words

Proposed Finality

When my autumn leaves loose color
And finally rest in God's sweet ground
Life's vagaries and wonders taken
With heart and soul are bound

To the gifts of beauty accepted
Beyond the golden days when
Life and love were plentiful
Even those passing away again

No summation alone can cover
The conscience over time
Complexity it's very nature
Perhaps, only God knows mine?

Although a heart full of wonder
With the pen-strokes love thrown out
In a wide swath of endearment
In my soft voice and not a shout

Not a saint this armor covers
But, the languish of a love in flux
Where a smile or laugh elicits
A temperance, perhaps my veil or crust!

No good bye's are forever
Yet, the time for all must come
Where the travel has been long and lovely
Holding all with love—some to special one's

My last Elizabeth is my gem
And, a golden heart I leave her
To fill her days with love
And, the smile she could always bring

The ambivalence of life
Caught in the spectra
Of inadequacy, strength, love,
Chance, luck, and softness

Love, even elicit love not taken
Was the soul of my being
Known, or unknown
It is still a world shaken

Accepted or rejected in context
Rejection should not enter
The labyrinth of the minds
Grey matter of depth

It will most probably be said:
That I wrote, but little else
A truism, yet a single tear,
A laugh, or a bright smile, is a legacy

My languish of thought
Was a hidden wealth of endearment
With a pen's smooth brush
I painted loves smooth rush

William E. Dickinson
A painter of words

Transient Breath

Life is so transient
As breath hovers in the wind
Blown about in beauty
Or, taken away to send

To our God almighty
As the hollow lungs do fill
Only with his anthems
Sung on heavens hills

Although we are blessed
On the seacoast of our shores
Where God alone does send us
To be with his love for evermore

On all our different journeys
Some short as transient breath
Most filled with love
As drop of sand on beaches crest

His breath of love takes over
In the silence of up above
Where we all will rest eternal
In the grandeur of God's love

William E. Dickinson
A painter of words
October 13, 2009 Noon

VENUES OF TIME

Angels Cry

The sap of life is diminished
When a drop of love is gone
With the choirs of heaven muted
Some will falter on

And sit upon their melted hopes
Diminutive in the hands of fate
Her gorgeous beaconing empty
Finding a friend in loves wake

A friend—not to cry in anguish
Nor to seed the flood
But, a partner in another skin
Can keep the heart in blood

Most sobbing sounds have vanished
From the sky and heavens above
Though a trickling tear may still be seen
When left with only lost love

They dry in Angel fashion
In the hitherto unknown
In that vast expanse of magic
When Christ is found at home

William E. Dickinson
A painter of words
May Day, 09

Fires Of Hell, and Other Light Topics

The fires of hell flame
Well beyond the night
The smell consumes the soul
All angels are in flight

The lonely hearts do suffer
The fate of all mankind
Life's vein running through
To all others now is blind

A persons soul so sacred
Managed by man and God
Unable the font to find
Therein lies the rod

In the towers of life we stumble
On the sands of the Sahara we die
The streams of life roll over us
And, on the bed we make, we lie

Associations in a time warp
Health on a plain
Dysfunction fully managed
And, we are but our name

Yet, beauty all around to see
Natures page is heavenly
Humans comprise mostly good
Trying to be understood

Ambitions all but over
We claim that is surely so
Though if talents bumble out
A lighter world we know

With a helping hand upon us
Infractions seem so small
And, we in turn support the same
Then all will have a ball

To end this dirge in pantomime
I'll sit and listen when
The Poet _____ before and next _____
A poem the world to send

William E. Dickinson
A painter of words
March 22, 2009

Flowering Moonbeam

I leach the field of emeralds
In my soulful heart
Beyond my ken to harvest
This foolish soul won't part

The antonym is playing soft
A theme I don't know
Beyond a Brahmin's wishes
My wandering does flow

Down the unknown highway
That one in the stars
This galaxy of mixed emotions
Mostly from the heart

The slipping of a moonbeam
Beyond the darkest cloud
As a familiar objects passing
Like a little bird in a crowd

Holding hands at midnight
With a fairy tale of naught
Slipping through the mind's filter
Into another vestige caught

A flowery grave awaits the dream
Which settles on light air
This floating not steadfast
Its calling is not heard

William E. Dickinson
A painter of words
June 01, 2009/Midnight

Haunting Melodies

Held in the arms of fate
My deadening soul clings on
Wholly owned and trampled
The blood of heart gasping from . . .

Pleading for grasp of tranquility
Flooding earnestness semi-controlled
Silences deafening amputates
Waned and fleecing goals

A fool and what are parted
Hope surrounding the sun
Eyes closed to perspective
Solutions soon undone

Why? The dark horse gallops!
Where the final line?
A card game of amnesia
Why the haunting refrain?

Healing hands all around
Yet, the stilt of mime remains
The end a haunting melody
Where anthems of stone now claim

William E. Dickinson
A painter of sad words
July 25, 2009

Lambent Connections

The strings of connection
Slip, slip, slipping away
Into the mist of memories archives
Solid foundations emerged in past

Is a poet's truth reality?
Where hopes and aspirations
Become the dreams of the soul
And the tenets of fantasy overwhelm

Do hopes and wants, and needs
Invite destiny as a myth, or a flower?
To grow as imagined dream
Or, to grow as needs profess?

These silken threads
The mind endeavors to hold
Succinct or blurry connections
To the needs memory engenders to unfold?

August attractions of loving in remorse
Mind unable to server loves history
The folds of time closing in
On the living memorials love professes
These lambent connections still shinning

William E. Dickinson
A painter of words

Time The Healer

What is oft the passage?
This thing, which we all take
Over and over we see it pass
With a tear, a hug, and even fate

Why is it so important?
This journey we have but one
Where the individual is unique
It is always one on one

Where the eye is on it
Or, avoidance is the game
Regardless of the outcome
To burn it is only our flame

When first the question is answered
For, the jotting is well to note
So small a digit is good to take
Forever we would like to cope

How it was expended
Is really not a crime?
But, value in a life well made
Is how we all should spend our time?

William E. Dickinson
A painter of words

Get Published, Inc!
Thorofare, NJ 08086
05 February, 2010
BA2010036